THE COMPLETE COFFEE COOKBOOK

42 Delicious Easy Coffee Recipes To Make Iced Coffee, Espresso Drink And More With BONUS 12 Coffee Based Desserts To Make At Home

EVE BRUNY

Would you like to know more about Small Batch Baking. I have a comprehensive guide to the Small Batch Baking Delight Cookbook. CLICK HERE TO ACCESS THE BOOK

Would you like to learn more about Special Appliance Cooking. I have complete comprehensive guide to the Air Fryer Bake Cookbook. CLICK HERE TO ACCESS THE BOOK

CONTENTS

THE
COMPLETE
COFFEE
COOKBOOK
42

Delicious Easy Coffee Recipes To
Make Iced Coffee, Espresso Drink
And More To Make At Home

BOUNS

12 COFFEE-BASED
DESSERTS

EVE BRUNY

INTRODUCTION

*I*n a world where mornings unfold with the alluring scent of freshly brewed coffee, where the simple act of holding a warm mug brings comfort and anticipation, lies a realm of endless possibilities. Welcome to **"The Complete Coffee Cookbook,"** a gateway to a sensory adventure like no other.

Imagine yourself in a bustling café, the air filled with the symphony of clinking cups and gentle chatter. Amidst this delightful chaos, you take a seat and order a cup of coffee. As the barista skillfully crafts your drink, your anticipation grows. The moment arrives—your first sip. A whirlwind of flavors dances on your tongue, captivating your taste buds and awakening your senses. It is in this moment that the magic of coffee reveals itself, enticing you to explore its depths further.

"The Complete Coffee Cookbook" invites you to embark on a journey through the captivating world of coffee. Within these pages, you will discover a treasure trove of knowledge, techniques, and recipes that will elevate your coffee experience to extraordinary heights. From the classic favorites that have stood the test of time to innovative creations that push the boundaries of flavor, this book serves as your compass on this aromatic voyage.

Beyond the enchantment of a single cup, coffee's versatility knows no bounds. Within its depths lie tantalizing secrets waiting to be unraveled. In this cookbook, we will not only delve into the art of brewing the perfect cup, but also explore the artistry of infusing coffee into delightful desserts, savory dishes, and even captivating cocktails.

From velvety tiramisu to robust coffee-rubbed meats, each recipe showcases coffee's ability to transform ordinary dishes into extraordinary culinary masterpieces.

In the **BONUS** section, we present a collection of irresistible coffee-infused desserts that will awaken your taste buds and leave you craving more. Each recipe is a testament to the artistry of combining the robust essence of coffee with the lusciousness of desserts.

"The Complete Coffee Cookbook" is not just for the seasoned coffee connoisseur; it is a guide for anyone eager to explore the world of coffee. Whether you are taking your first steps into this aromatic realm or seeking to expand your knowledge, this book will be your trusted companion. It will equip you with the tools, techniques, and understanding to become a coffee maestro in your own right.

So, dear reader, prepare to awaken your senses and embark on a voyage of aromatic delights. Whether you are savoring a quiet morning moment, hosting a gathering of friends, or delighting in the art of culinary creation, let **"The Complete Coffee Cookbook"** be your gateway to unlocking the full potential of this magical elixir. Together, let us discover the boundless wonders that lie within a single bean, and let our shared love for coffee weave a tapestry of unforgettable moments and flavors.

*I*ndulge in the captivating realm of coffee mastery, where each step unfolds a sensory experience beyond comparison. The Art of Brewing Coffee is a captivating ritual that transcends the ordinary, transforming the mere act of making a beverage into a journey of pleasure and refinement.

Understanding Coffee Beans opens the doors to a world of untapped potential. These remarkable little seeds hold within them a treasure trove of flavors, waiting to be released. By delving into their origins, embracing their distinct characteristics, and savoring the stories they tell, you embark on an adventure that will forever change your perception of this beloved brew.

Coffee Grinding Techniques are the key to unlocking a symphony of aromas and tastes. With every turn of the grinder, you unleash a whirlwind of fragrant notes, awakening the senses and setting the stage for a truly exquisite cup of coffee. The grind size, meticulously chosen, holds the power to create a brew that is rich, bold, or delicate, depending on your desires.

*B*rewing Methods and Equipment are the artisans that shape your coffee experience. From the sleek elegance of a pour-over to the intense precision of an espresso machine, these tools of the trade give life to your vision. They empower you to sculpt the flavors, the body, and the character of your brew, transforming each cup into a masterpiece to be savored.

Choosing the Right Water is an often overlooked secret to achieving coffee nirvana. Just as an artist selects the finest pigments for their canvas, you must choose water that is pure, pristine, and attuned to the delicate alchemy of coffee brewing. This vital element can enhance the flavors, elevate the nuances, and elevate your brew to new heights of perfection.

Perfecting the Coffee-to-Water Ratio is the alchemical formula that turns mere ingredients into liquid gold. Balancing the strength and subtleties of your brew requires precision and finesse. By understanding the science behind the ideal coffee-to-water ratio, you unlock the gateway to a symphony of flavors that dance harmoniously on your palate, leaving you craving for more.

*E*mbrace this journey of mastery, where every step is an invitation to indulge in the extraordinary. The Art of Brewing Coffee beckons you to explore the depths of your senses, to unlock the full potential of the humble bean, and to craft a cup of perfection that transcends the boundaries of the ordinary. Elevate your coffee experience, savor the delights of each sip, and join the league of connoisseurs who understand the magic that lies within the art of brewing coffee.

WHAT IS COFFEE

Coffee is a common brew made from roasted coffee beans, which are actually the Coffea plant's seeds.The most commonly used species of Coffea for producing coffee are arabica and Coffea canephora (also known as Robusta). The process of making coffee involves grinding the roasted beans and then brewing them with hot water to extract the flavors and aroma. Coffee can be consumed in various forms such as black coffee, espresso, cappuccino, latte, and many more, often customized with milk, sugar, or other additives according to personal preference.

Coffee and Health

The health effects of coffee have been a topic of extensive research and discussion. Overall, moderate coffee consumption is generally considered safe for most individuals, but its effects can vary depending on factors such as individual metabolism, overall health, and the amount consumed. It is important to note that excessive consumption or adding unhealthy ingredients like excessive sugar or creamers can have negative health consequences.

Coffee and Its Health Benefits:

Coffee has been associated with several potential health benefits, backed by scientific studies. Some of the notable health benefits of coffee include:

Antioxidant properties: Coffee is rich in antioxidants, such as chlorogenic acid and caffeine, which can help combat oxidative stress in the body and reduce the risk of chronic diseases.

Improved cognitive function: The caffeine in coffee can enhance alertness, concentration, and cognitive performance. It may also help reduce the risk of neurodegenerative disorders like Alzheimer's and Parkinson's diseases.

Liver protection: Moderate coffee consumption has been linked to a reduced risk of liver diseases, including liver cirrhosis, liver cancer, and non-alcoholic fatty liver disease (NAFLD).

Reduced risk of certain diseases: Regular coffee consumption has been associated with a lower risk of conditions such as type 2 diabetes, cardiovascular diseases, certain types of cancers (such as liver and colorectal cancer), and stroke.

Improved physical performance: Caffeine in coffee acts as a stimulant and can enhance physical performance, endurance, and muscle strength. It may also help in fat burning and improving athletic performance.

Antioxidants in Coffee:

The normal Western diet includes a lot of coffee as an important source of antioxidants. Antioxidants are compounds that help neutralize harmful free radicals in the body, thereby protecting cells from damage and reducing the risk of chronic diseases. Chlorogenic acid, a major antioxidant found in coffee, is believed to contribute to its beneficial effects on health. Other antioxidants present in coffee include caffeic acid, quinines, and polyphenols.

Effects of Coffee on Brain Function:

Coffee is a popular beverage consumed worldwide due to its stimulating effects, primarily attributed to its high caffeine content. The following are some of the effects of coffee on brain function:

Alertness and Cognitive Performance: Caffeine, the main active component in coffee, acts as a central nervous system stimulant. It blocks the adenosine receptors in the brain, which helps to increase alertness and reduce fatigue. By doing so, coffee can improve various aspects of cognitive performance, such as attention, reaction time, memory, and overall mental acuity.

Mood Enhancement: Coffee consumption has been associated with an improvement in mood and a decrease in depressive symptoms. Caffeine stimulates the release of neurotransmitters like dopamine, serotonin, and norepinephrine, which are involved in regulating mood and promoting feelings of well-being.

Enhanced Focus and Concentration: Coffee can enhance focus and concentration by increasing the production of neurotransmitters like dopamine and norepinephrine, which are involved in regulating attention and focus. This can be

13

particularly beneficial during tasks that require sustained mental effort.

Memory and Learning: Caffeine has been found to have a positive impact on memory and learning. It may enhance memory consolidation, which is the process of converting short-term memories into long-term memories. This effect is especially noticeable for tasks that require the retrieval of information from memory.

Neuroprotective Effects: Coffee contains various antioxidants and bioactive compounds that have been associated with potential neuroprotective effects. Regular coffee consumption has been linked to a reduced risk of neurodegenerative diseases such as Alzheimer's and Parkinson's. To completely understand the underlying mechanisms, more study is necessary.

Headache Relief: Caffeine is a common ingredient in many over-the-counter headache medications due to its ability to constrict blood vessels and alleviate pain. In moderate amounts, coffee consumption may provide relief from certain types of headaches and migraines.

It's important to note that individual responses to coffee can vary based on factors such as genetics, tolerance, and overall health. Additionally, excessive consumption of coffee or caffeine can lead to negative effects like anxiety, insomnia, and jitteriness. Moderation is key when it comes to reaping the potential benefits of coffee on brain function.

Coffee and Metabolism:

Coffee has been studied for its potential effects on metabolism, including its impact on energy expenditure, fat oxidation, and insulin sensitivity. Here are some key points regarding coffee and metabolism:

Increased Energy Expenditure: Caffeine, present in coffee, has thermogenic properties, meaning it can increase the body's energy expenditure. This effect occurs through the stimulation of the sympathetic nervous system, leading to an increase in heart rate and metabolic rate. However, the magnitude of this effect is relatively small and may vary among individuals.

Fat Oxidation: Coffee consumption has been associated with enhanced fat oxidation, which is the body's ability to break down fat for energy. Caffeine can stimulate the release of free fatty acids from fat tissue, making them available for use as an energy source. This can potentially contribute to weight loss or weight maintenance when combined with a balanced diet and regular physical activity.

Appetite Suppression: Coffee has been reported to have appetite-suppressing effects, which may help in reducing calorie intake. The exact mechanisms behind this effect are not fully understood but may involve the interaction of caffeine with certain receptors in the brain that regulate hunger and satiety.

Insulin Sensitivity: Some studies suggest that coffee consumption, particularly caffeinated coffee, may improve insulin sensitivity. Insulin is a hormone responsible for regulating blood sugar levels, and increased sensitivity to insulin can help prevent the development of type 2 diabetes. However, more research is needed.

Coffee-inspired Breakfast and Brunch

1.Coffee Pancakes

Ingredients

1 cup all-purpose flour

2 tablespoons sugar

2 teaspoons baking powder

1/2 teaspoon salt

1 cup milk

1/4 cup brewed coffee, cooled

1 large egg

2 tablespoons unsalted butter, melted

1 teaspoon vanilla extract

Preparation

Mix the flour, sugar, baking soda, and salt in a sizable bowl.

Combine the milk, coffee that has been made, egg, melted butter, and vanilla essence in a different bowl.

After adding the liquid components, mix the dry ingredients only until they are barely blended. Avoid overmixing, a few lumps are acceptable.

Heat a non-stick griddle or skillet over medium heat and lightly grease with butter or cooking spray.

For each pancake, pour 1/4 cup of batter onto the griddle.

Cook until bubbles form on the surface of the pancake, then flip and cook for another 1-2 minutes, until golden brown.

Serve the coffee pancakes warm with your favorite toppings such as maple syrup, whipped cream, or fresh berries.

2.Coffee Smoothie Bowl

Ingredients

1 frozen banana

1/2 cup brewed coffee, chilled

1/2 cup unsweetened almond milk (or milk of your choice)

2 tablespoons rolled oats

1 tablespoon of your preferred nut butter, such as almond butter

1 tablespoon honey or maple syrup (optional)

Toppings of your choice: sliced banana, granola, chia seeds, shredded coconut, etc.

Preparation

In a blender, combine the frozen banana, brewed coffee, almond milk, rolled oats, almond butter, and honey or maple syrup (if desired).

Blend until smooth and creamy, adding more almond milk if needed to reach your desired consistency.

Pour the smoothie into a bowl.

Top with your favorite toppings such as sliced banana, granola, chia seeds, or shredded coconut.

Enjoy your coffee smoothie bowl with a spoon and savor the coffee-infused goodness.

3.Coffee Oatmeal

Ingredients

1 cup rolled oats

1 cup brewed coffee, cooled

1 cup milk (dairy or plant-based)

1 tablespoon honey or maple syrup (optional)

1/2 teaspoon vanilla extract

Pinch of salt

Toppings of your choice: sliced almonds, dried fruit, cinnamon, etc.

Preparation

In a saucepan, combine the rolled oats, brewed coffee, milk, honey or maple syrup (if desired), vanilla extract, and salt.

Over medium heat, whisk the mixture occasionally as it simmers gently.

Cook for about 5 minutes or until the oats have absorbed the liquid and reached your desired consistency.

Remove from heat and let it sit for a minute.

Serve the coffee oatmeal warm in bowls and top with your favorite toppings such as sliced almonds, dried fruit, or a sprinkle of cinnamon.

4.Coffee Muffins

Ingredients

2 cups all-purpose flour

1/2 cup granulated sugar

2 teaspoons baking powder

1/2 teaspoon baking soda

1/4 teaspoon salt

1 cup brewed coffee, cooled

1/2 cup unsalted butter, melted

1/4 cup milk

1 large egg

1 teaspoon vanilla extract

Preparation

Preheat your oven to 375°F (190°C) and line a muffin tin with paper liners.

Mix the flour, sugar, baking soda, baking powder, and salt in a big bowl.

In a separate bowl, combine the brewed coffee, melted butter, milk, egg, and vanilla extract.

After adding the liquid components, mix the dry ingredients only until they are barely blended. Avoid overmixing, a few lumps are acceptable.

Evenly distribute the batter among the muffin tins, filling each one about two-thirds full.

Optional: Sprinkle some additional sugar or a dusting of cinnamon on top for added flavor and texture.

A toothpick put into the center of a muffin should come out clean after 18 to 20 minutes of baking in a preheated oven.

Remove from the oven and allow the muffins to cool in the pan for a few minutes before transferring them to a wire rack to cool completely.

Enjoy the coffee-infused muffins as a delightful breakfast or snack.

5.Coffee Granola
Ingredients

3 cups old-fashioned rolled oats

1 cup chopped nuts (e.g., almonds, walnuts, or pecans)

1/2 cup unsweetened shredded coconut

1/4 cup ground flaxseed

1/4 cup honey or maple syrup

1/4 cup brewed coffee, cooled

2 tablespoons coconut oil, melted

1 teaspoon vanilla extract

1/2 teaspoon ground cinnamon

Pinch of salt

Optional: dried fruit (e.g., raisins, cranberries, or apricots).

Preparation

Preheat your oven to 325°F (163°C) and line a baking sheet with parchment paper.

In a large bowl, combine the rolled oats, chopped nuts, shredded coconut, ground flaxseed, cinnamon, and salt.

In a separate bowl, whisk together the honey or maple syrup, brewed coffee, melted coconut oil, and vanilla extract.

Pour the wet ingredients over the dry ingredients and stir until well coated.

Spread the granola mixture evenly onto the prepared baking sheet.

Bake in the preheated oven for 20-25 minutes, stirring halfway through, until the granola is golden brown and fragrant.

Optional: Add dried fruit to the granola once it has cooled.

Allow the granola to cool completely on the baking sheet before transferring it to an airtight container for storage.

Enjoy the coffee-infused granola as a crunchy topping for yogurt, a nutritious snack, or a flavorful addition to your breakfast bowls.

6.Coffee Chia Pudding

Ingredients

1/4 cup chia seeds

1 cup brewed coffee, cooled

1 cup milk (dairy or plant-based)

2 tablespoons honey or maple syrup

1/2 teaspoon vanilla extract

Optional toppings: sliced almonds, chocolate shavings, fresh berries, etc.

Preparation

In a bowl or jar, combine the chia seeds, brewed coffee, milk, honey or maple syrup, and vanilla extract.

Stir well to ensure the chia seeds are evenly distributed and not clumping together.

Cover the bowl or jar and refrigerate for at least 4 hours or overnight, allowing the chia seeds to absorb the liquid and create a pudding-like consistency.

Stir the mixture a couple of times during the first hour to prevent clumping.

Once the chia pudding has set, give it a final stir and adjust the sweetness if desired.

Serve the coffee chia pudding in individual bowls or jars, and top with your favorite toppings such as sliced almonds, chocolate shavings, fresh berries, or any other desired toppings.

Enjoy the coffee-infused chia pudding as a delightful and nutritious breakfast or snack.

7.Coffee French Toast

Ingredients

4 slices of bread (preferably brioche or French bread)

2 large eggs

1/2 cup milk

1/4 cup brewed coffee, cooled

1 tablespoon granulated sugar

1/2 teaspoon vanilla extract

Pinch of salt

For frying pan greasing, use butter or cooking spray.

Optional toppings: powdered sugar, maple syrup, whipped cream, fresh berries

Preparation

In a shallow bowl, whisk together the eggs, milk, brewed coffee, granulated sugar, vanilla extract, and salt until well combined.

Grease a non-stick skillet or griddle with butter or cooking spray before heating it over medium heat.

Dip each slice of bread into the coffee-egg mixture, allowing it to soak for a few seconds on each side.

Slices of soaked bread should be placed into a warm skillet or griddle and fried for two to three minutes on each side, or until golden and cooked through.

Remove the French toast from the pan and repeat with the remaining slices of bread.

Serve the coffee-infused French toast warm with your favorite toppings such as a dusting of powdered sugar, a drizzle of maple syrup, a dollop of whipped cream, or fresh berries.

8.Coffee Breakfast Smoothie

Ingredients

1 ripe banana

1/2 cup brewed coffee, cooled

1/2 cup Greek yogurt

1/2 cup milk (dairy or plant-based)

1 tablespoon almond butter or peanut butter

1 tablespoon of optionally sweetened honey or maple syrup

1/2 teaspoon vanilla extract

1 cup ice cubes

Preparation:

Place all the ingredients in a blender.

If necessary, add more milk to change the consistency of the mixture until it is smooth and creamy.

If more sweetness is wanted, add honey or maple syrup after tasting the smoothie.

Pour the coffee breakfast smoothie into a glass and enjoy it as a satisfying and energizing start to your day.

9. Coffee Overnight Oats

Ingredients

1/2 cup rolled oats

1/2 cup brewed coffee, cooled

1/2 cup milk (dairy or plant-based)

1 tablespoon chia seeds

1 tablespoon honey or maple syrup

1/2 teaspoon vanilla extract

Optional toppings: sliced almonds, fresh berries, shredded coconut, etc.

Preparation

In a jar or container with a lid, combine the rolled oats, brewed coffee, milk, chia seeds, honey or maple syrup, and vanilla extract.

Make sure all the ingredients are fully combined by giving them a good stir.

Refrigerate the jar/container overnight or for at least 4 hours to allow the oats to soften and absorb the liquid. Cover the jar/container with the lid.

Give the coffee overnight oats a thorough toss in the morning.

Add your desired toppings such as sliced almonds, fresh berries, or shredded coconut.

Enjoy the convenient and delicious coffee-infused overnight oats for a quick and nutritious breakfast on the go.

10.Coffee Breakfast Parfait

Ingredients

1 cup Greek yogurt

1/4 cup brewed coffee, cooled

2 tablespoons honey or maple syrup

1/2 teaspoon vanilla extract

1/2 cup granola

1/2 cup fresh berries or sliced fruit of your choice

Preparation

In a bowl, combine the Greek yogurt, brewed coffee, honey or maple syrup, and vanilla extract. Stir well to combine.

In a glass or jar, layer the coffee yogurt mixture with granola and fresh berries or sliced fruit.

Repeat the layers until all the ingredients are used, finishing with a layer of granola and fruit on top.

Optionally, drizzle some additional honey or maple syrup on the top for added sweetness.

Place the breakfast parfait in the refrigerator for at least 30 minutes to allow the flavors to meld together.

Serve the coffee breakfast parfait chilled and enjoy the delightful combination of creamy yogurt, crunchy granola, and bursts of fresh fruit.

Unique Coffee Blends

11.Mocha Java Blend

Ingredients

1/2 cup medium roast coffee beans

1/2 cup dark roast coffee beans

1 tablespoon cocoa powder

1 tablespoon finely ground dark chocolate

Preparation

Grind the medium roast and dark roast coffee beans separately until they reach a medium-coarse consistency.

In a bowl, combine the ground coffee beans, cocoa powder, and finely ground dark chocolate. Mix well.

Store the Mocha Java blend in an airtight container.

Brew the coffee using your preferred method, using approximately 1-2 tablespoons of the Mocha Java blend per 6 ounces of water.

Enjoy your flavorful Mocha Java coffee!

12.Hazelnut Caramel Fusion

Ingredients

1/2 cup medium roast coffee beans

1/4 cup hazelnuts, crushed

2 tablespoons caramel sauce

Preparation

Grind the medium roast coffee beans to a medium-fine consistency.

In a bowl, combine the ground coffee beans, crushed hazelnuts, and caramel sauce. Mix well.

Transfer the Hazelnut Caramel Fusion blend to an airtight container.

Brew the coffee using your preferred method, using approximately 1-2 tablespoons of the Hazelnut Caramel Fusion blend per 6 ounces of water.

Sit back, relax, and savor the delicious aroma of Hazelnut Caramel Fusion coffee!

13.Spiced Vanilla Espresso

Ingredients

1/2 cup espresso beans

1 teaspoon ground cinnamon

1/2 teaspoon vanilla extract

Preparation

Grind the espresso beans to a fine consistency.

In a small bowl, mix the ground espresso beans, ground cinnamon, and vanilla extract until well combined.

Transfer the Spiced Vanilla Espresso blend to an airtight container.

Brew the coffee using an espresso machine or moka pot, using approximately 1-2 tablespoons of the Spiced Vanilla Espresso blend per shot.

Indulge in the warm and aromatic flavors of Spiced Vanilla Espresso!

14.Maple Walnut Caramel
Ingredients

1/2 cup medium roast coffee beans

2 tablespoons maple syrup

1/4 cup chopped walnuts

1 tablespoon caramel sauce

Preparation

Grind the medium roast coffee beans to a medium-fine consistency.

In a bowl, combine the ground coffee beans, maple syrup, chopped walnuts, and caramel sauce. Mix well.

Store the Maple Walnut Caramel blend in an airtight container.

Brew the coffee using your preferred method, using approximately 1-2 tablespoons of the Maple Walnut Caramel blend per 6 ounces of water.

Sip and savor the delightful combination of maple, walnut, and caramel in every cup!

15.Dark Chocolate Raspberry

Ingredients

1/2 cup dark roast coffee beans

1 tablespoon cocoa powder

1 tablespoon freeze-dried raspberry powder

Preparation

Grind the dark roast coffee beans to a medium-coarse consistency.

In a bowl, combine the ground coffee beans, cocoa powder, and freeze-dried raspberry powder. Mix well.

Transfer the Dark Chocolate Raspberry blend to an airtight container.

Brew the coffee using your preferred method, using approximately 1-2 tablespoons of the Dark Chocolate Raspberry blend per 6 ounces of water.

Treat yourself to the rich and fruity taste of Dark Chocolate Raspberry coffee!

16.Caramelized Pecan Praline

Ingredients

1/2 cup medium roast coffee beans

1/4 cup pecans, chopped

2 tablespoons brown sugar

1 tablespoon caramel sauce

Preparation

The dark roast coffee beans should be ground to a medium-coarse texture.

In a small saucepan, heat the pecans over medium heat until toasted and fragrant. Remove from heat and set aside.

In the same saucepan, add the brown sugar and caramel sauce. Cook over medium heat, stirring constantly, until the sugar has melted and caramelized.

Add the toasted pecans to the caramel mixture and stir to coat the pecans evenly. Remove from heat and let cool.

In a bowl, combine the ground coffee beans and the cooled caramelized pecan mixture. Mix well.

Store the Caramelized Pecan Praline blend in an airtight container.

Brew the coffee using your preferred method, using approximately 1-2 tablespoons of the Caramelized Pecan Praline blend per 6 ounces of water.

Sit back and enjoy the delightful combination of caramel, pecans, and coffee in each sip.

Coffee Cocktails

17. Classic Espresso Martini
Ingredients

1 shot of espresso

1 1/2 shots of vodka

1/2 shot of coffee liqueur

1/2 shot of simple syrup

Ice cubes

Coffee beans (for garnish)

Preparation

Espresso should be made and allowed to cool.

Fill a cocktail shaker with ice cubes.

Add the vodka, coffee liqueur, cooled espresso, and simple syrup to the shaker.

For around 15 seconds, shake the mixture ferociously.

Strain the cocktail into a martini glass.

Add a few coffee beans as a garnish.

18.Irish Coffee

Ingredients

1 1/2 oz Irish whiskey

1 cup of hot brewed coffee

2 tsp brown sugar

Whipped cream (for topping)

Preparation

Make some coffee and keep it warm.

In a heat-resistant glass, dissolve the brown sugar in a small amount of hot water.

Add the Irish whiskey to the glass and stir to combine.

Pour the hot coffee into the glass and stir gently.

Add plenty of whipped cream on top of the coffee.

Optionally, you can dust some cocoa powder or sprinkle cinnamon on top of the whipped cream for extra flavor.

19.Coffee Old Fashioned

Ingredients

2 oz bourbon

1/2 oz coffee liqueur

2 dashes of Angostura bitters

1 sugar cube

Orange peel (for garnish)

Ice cubes

Preparation

In an old-fashioned glass, muddle the sugar cube with a few drops of water until it dissolves.

Add ice cubes to the glass.

Pour the bourbon, coffee liqueur, and Angostura bitters over the ice.

In order to blend the ingredients and chill the drink, stir slowly for 20 to 30 seconds.

Garnish with a twist of orange peel.

20.Coffee Negroni
Ingredients

1 oz coffee-infused gin

1 oz Campari

1 oz sweet vermouth

Orange peel (for garnish)

Ice cubes

Preparation

To infuse the gin, add coffee beans to a bottle of gin and let it sit for at least 24 hours. Strain out the coffee beans before using.

Fill a mixing glass with ice cubes.

Add the coffee-infused gin, Campari, and sweet vermouth to the glass.

Stir gently for about 20-30 seconds to mix the ingredients and chill the drink.

Pour the cocktail through a strainer into an ice-filled rocks glass.

Garnish with a twist of orange peel.

21.Coffee Mojito
Ingredients

2 oz rum

1 oz coffee liqueur

1 oz fresh lime juice

8-10 fresh mint leaves

1 tsp sugar

Club soda

Ice cubes

Lime slices and mint sprigs (for garnish)

Preparation

Mint leaves and sugar should be combined in a cocktail shaker.

Add the rum, coffee liqueur, and lime juice to the shaker.

Fill the shaker with ice cubes.

Shake the mixture ferociously for 15 seconds total.

Put the cocktail through a strainer into an ice-filled glass.

Top with club soda.

Garnish with lime slices and mint sprigs.

Espresso-based Drinks

22.Classic Espresso Shot

Ingredients

1 shot of espresso

Preparation

Grind fresh coffee beans to a fine consistency.

Pack the ground coffee tightly into the espresso machine's portafilter.

Attach the portafilter to the espresso machine.

Place an espresso cup under the portafilter.

Start the espresso machine and let the water pass through the coffee grounds to extract the espresso shot.

The shot should take approximately 25-30 seconds to extract.

Once the shot is complete, remove the cup and serve the espresso immediately.

23.Cappuccino

Ingredients

1 shot of espresso

1/3 cup of steamed milk

1/3 cup of foamed milk

Cocoa powder or cinnamon (optional, for garnish)

Preparation

Prepare a shot of espresso using the method described in the Classic Espresso Shot recipe.

Steam the milk using a milk frother or steam wand until it reaches a temperature of around 150°F (65°C).

Pour the steamed milk into a cup, holding back the foam with a spoon.

Add the espresso shot to the cup with steamed milk.

Spoon the foam from the steamed milk on top of the drink.

Optional: Dust the foam with cocoa powder or cinnamon for garnish.

Serve the cappuccino immediately.

24.Latte
Ingredients

1 shot of espresso

1 cup of steamed milk

Milk foam

Preparation

Prepare a shot of espresso using the method described in the Classic Espresso Shot recipe.

Steam the milk using a milk frother or steam wand until it reaches a temperature of around 150°F (65°C).

Pour the steamed milk into a cup, holding back the foam with a spoon.

Add the espresso shot to the cup with steamed milk.

Spoon a layer of milk foam on top of the drink.

Serve the latte immediately.

25.Macchiato
Ingredients

1 shot of espresso

A dollop of foamed milk

Preparation

Prepare a shot of espresso using the method described in the Classic Espresso Shot recipe.

Steam the milk using a milk frother or steam wand until it reaches a temperature of around 150°F (65°C).

In a tiny cup, pour the espresso shot.

Add a dollop of foamed milk on top of the espresso shot.

Serve the macchiato immediately.

26. Mocha

Ingredients

1 shot of espresso

1 tablespoon of cocoa powder

1 tablespoon of sugar

1 cup of steamed milk

Whipped cream (optional, for topping)

Chocolate shavings (optional, for garnish)

Preparation

Prepare a shot of espresso using the method described in the Classic Espresso Shot recipe.

In a small saucepan, mix the cocoa powder and sugar with a small amount of hot water to form a paste.

Heat the saucepan over medium heat, stirring constantly until the mixture is smooth and well combined.

Add the espresso shot to the saucepan and stir until fully incorporated.

Pour the mixture into a cup.

Steam the milk using a milk frother or steam wand until it reaches a temperature of around 150°F (65°C).

Pour the steamed milk into the cup with the espresso and cocoa mixture.

Optional: Top with whipped cream and sprinkle with chocolate shavings for garnish.

Serve the mocha immediately.

27. Americano

Ingredients

1 shot of espresso

Hot water

Preparation

Prepare a shot of espresso using the method described in the Classic Espresso Shot recipe.

Fill a cup or mug halfway with hot water.

Add the espresso shot to the cup with hot water.

Mix the boiling water and espresso with a gentle stir.

Serve the Americano immediately.

Note: The strength of an Americano can be adjusted by adding more or less hot water, depending on personal preference.

Milk-based Drinks

28.Café au Lait

Ingredients

1 cup brewed coffee

1 cup milk

Sugar (optional)

Preparation

Brew a cup of coffee according to your preference.

The milk should be heated in a small pan over medium heat until it is warm but not boiling.

Froth the milk using a frother or whisk vigorously until it becomes frothy and has a velvety texture.

Pour the hot coffee into a mug and slowly pour the frothed milk on top.

Add sugar if desired and stir gently to combine.

Serve immediately.

29.Flat White

Ingredients

1 shot of espresso

6 ounces steamed milk

Microfoam (optional)

Preparation

Use an espresso machine to brew a shot of espresso.

In a separate container, steam the milk until it reaches a velvety texture with microfoam. The milk ought to be warm but not boiling.

Pour the steamed milk slowly over the espresso shot, holding back the foam with a spoon to create a layered effect.

If desired, spoon a small amount of microfoam on top of the drink for latte art or additional foam.

Serve immediately.

30.Cortado
Ingredients

1 shot of espresso

1 ounce steamed milk

Preparation

Use an espresso machine to brew a shot of espresso.

In a separate container, steam the milk until it reaches a velvety texture.

Pour the steamed milk into a glass, filling it about halfway.

Slowly pour the espresso shot into the glass, aiming to maintain a 1:1 ratio of espresso to milk.

Serve immediately.

31.Affogato
Ingredients

1 scoop of vanilla gelato or ice cream

1 shot of hot espresso

Preparation

Place a scoop of vanilla ice cream or gelato in a serving dish or glass.

Use an espresso machine to brew a shot of espresso.

Over the ice cream, pour the hot espresso shot.

Allow the espresso to melt the ice cream slightly before serving.

Serve immediately, optionally garnishing with chocolate shavings or a sprinkle of cocoa powder.

32.Breve

Ingredients

1 shot of espresso

6 ounces steamed half-and-half or cream

Preparation

Use an espresso machine to brew a shot of espresso.

In a separate container, steam the half-and-half or cream until it reaches a velvety texture.

Pour the steamed half-and-half or cream slowly over the espresso shot, holding back the foam with a spoon to create a layered effect.

Serve immediately.

Iced Coffee Delights

33.Iced Coffee Delights

Ingredients

1 cup strong brewed coffee

Ice cubes

Sweetener (sugar, honey, or flavored syrup)

Milk or cream (optional)

Whipped cream (optional)

Chocolate syrup or sprinkles (optional)

Preparation

Strong coffee should be made and allowed to cool.

Fill a glass with ice cubes.

Pour the cooled coffee over the ice cubes.

Add sweetener according to your taste preferences and stir well.

If desired, add milk or cream to the iced coffee and stir again.

Top it off with whipped cream and drizzle chocolate syrup or sprinkle some chocolate shavings for an extra touch of indulgence (optional).

Serve and enjoy your Iced Coffee Delight!

34.Iced Coffee Basics

Ingredients

1 cup brewed coffee

Ice cubes

Sugar or sweetener (optional)

Milk or cream (optional)

Preparation

Your preferred coffee should be brewed, then allowed to cool.

Fill a glass with ice cubes.

Pour the cooled coffee over the ice cubes.

Add sugar or sweetener if desired and stir well until dissolved.

If desired, add milk or cream to the iced coffee and stir again.

Adjust the sweetness and creaminess according to your taste.

35.Cold Brew Concentrate

Ingredients

1 cup coarsely ground coffee

4 cups cold water

Preparation

Place the coarsely ground coffee in a large jar or pitcher.

Pour the cold water over the coffee grounds, ensuring that all the grounds are fully saturated.

Stir gently to make sure the coffee grounds are fully mixed with the water.

Cover the jar or pitcher and let it steep at room temperature for 12 to 24 hours.

After steeping, filter the coffee concentrate to remove the grounds using a fine-mesh sieve or coffee filter.

Transfer the cold brew concentrate to a clean container or bottle and refrigerate until ready to use.

To serve, dilute the concentrate with water or milk, and add ice cubes if desired.

Enjoy your smooth and bold Cold Brew Concentrate!

36.Classic Iced Coffee

Ingredients

1 cup brewed coffee

Ice cubes

Sugar or sweetener (optional)

Milk or cream (optional)

Preparation

Make some coffee, then let it cool.

Fill a glass with ice cubes.

Pour the cooled coffee over the ice cubes.

Add sugar or sweetener to taste and stir well until dissolved.

If desired, add milk or cream to the iced coffee and stir again.

You can adjust the sweetness and creaminess to your liking.

Serve and enjoy your Classic Iced Coffee!

37. Vietnamese Iced Coffee

Ingredients

2 tablespoons coarsely ground coffee (preferably dark roast)

2 tablespoons sweetened condensed milk

Ice cubes

Preparation

Place the coarsely ground coffee in a Vietnamese coffee filter or a drip coffee maker.

Set the coffee filter over a glass or a mug.

Pour a small amount of hot water (about 1/4 cup) into the coffee filter to moisten the grounds, then let it drip for a minute.

Add the remaining hot water (about 3/4 cup) and let it drip through slowly.

Once all the coffee has dripped through, remove the coffee filter.

Fill a glass with ice cubes.

Over the ice cubes, pour the brewed coffee.

Add the sweetened condensed milk to the glass with ice cubes.

Stir well until the condensed milk is fully blended with the coffee.

Adjust the sweetness and creaminess by adding more condensed milk if desired.

Serve and enjoy your authentic Vietnamese Iced Coffee!

38.Frappuccino

Ingredients

1 cup strong brewed coffee, chilled

1 cup milk

1/4 cup granulated sugar

1 cup ice cubes

Whipped cream (optional)

Chocolate syrup or caramel sauce (optional)

Preparation

Brew a cup of strong coffee and let it cool completely.

In a blender, combine the chilled coffee, milk, granulated sugar, and ice cubes.

Blend everything at a high speed until the frappuccino is smooth and the ingredients are well combined.

Pour the frappuccino into a glass.

If desired, top it off with whipped cream and drizzle some chocolate syrup or caramel sauce.

Serve immediately and enjoy your refreshing Frappuccino!

39.Iced Mocha

Ingredients

1 cup brewed coffee, cooled

1/2 cup milk

2 tablespoons chocolate syrup

Ice cubes

Whipped cream (optional)

Chocolate shavings or cocoa powder (optional)

Preparation

Make some coffee, then let it cool.

In a glass, combine the cooled coffee, milk, and chocolate syrup.

Stir well until the chocolate syrup is fully incorporated into the mixture.

Fill the glass with ice cubes.

If desired, top it off with whipped cream and sprinkle some chocolate shavings or cocoa powder.

Give it a final stir and enjoy your indulgent Iced Mocha!

Coffee-infused Sauces and Syrups

40.Coffee BBQ Sauce

Ingredients

1 cup ketchup

1/2 cup brewed coffee

1/4 cup brown sugar

2 tablespoons apple cider vinegar

2 tablespoons Worcestershire sauce

1 tablespoon Dijon mustard

1 tablespoon molasses

1 teaspoon smoked paprika

1/2 teaspoon garlic powder

1/2 teaspoon onion powder

1/2 teaspoon salt

1/4 teaspoon black pepper

Preparation

In a saucepan, combine all the ingredients: ketchup, brewed coffee, brown sugar, apple cider vinegar, Worcestershire sauce, Dijon mustard, molasses, smoked paprika, garlic powder, onion powder, salt, and black pepper.

Whisk the ingredients together until well combined.

Bring the mixture to a simmer in the saucepan over medium heat.

Reduce the heat to low and let the sauce simmer for about 15-20 minutes, stirring occasionally, until it thickens to your desired consistency.

The sauce should be taken off the stove and allowed to cool.

Transfer the Coffee BBQ Sauce to a jar or airtight container.

For up to two weeks, keep in the fridge.

41.Coffee Caramel Sauce

Ingredients

1 cup granulated sugar

1/4 cup water

1/2 cup heavy cream

1/4 cup brewed coffee

2 tablespoons unsalted butter

1/2 teaspoon vanilla extract

Pinch of salt

Preparation

In a medium saucepan, combine the granulated sugar and water.

Place the saucepan over medium heat and stir until the sugar dissolves.

Without stirring, let the mixture come to a boil. Continue boiling until the syrup turns into a deep amber color.

Remove the saucepan from heat and carefully add the heavy cream. Be cautious as the mixture will bubble vigorously.

Stir in the brewed coffee, unsalted butter, vanilla extract, and a pinch of salt.

Return the saucepan to low heat and whisk the mixture until the caramel sauce is smooth and well combined.

Cook the sauce for an additional 2-3 minutes, stirring constantly.

Take it off the fire and give it a minute to cool.

Transfer the Coffee Caramel Sauce to a jar or airtight container.

For up to two weeks, keep in the fridge.

42.Coffee-flavored Dessert Syrups

Ingredients

1 cup water

1 cup granulated sugar

1/4 cup brewed coffee

1 teaspoon vanilla extract

Preparation

In a small saucepan, combine water and granulated sugar.

Place the saucepan over medium heat and stir until the sugar dissolves completely.

The mixture should be gently brought to a boil before being simmered for 5 minutes.

Remove the saucepan from heat and stir in the brewed coffee and vanilla extract.

Let the syrup cool down before transferring it to a bottle or jar.

Store the Coffee-flavored Dessert Syrup in the refrigerator for up to two weeks.

Use it to drizzle over pancakes, waffles, ice cream, or any other dessert of your choice.

Bonus: 12 Coffee based desserts

1.Coffee Chocolate Mousse

Ingredients

1 cup heavy cream

1/4 cup brewed coffee, cooled

8 ounces dark chocolate, chopped

3 tablespoons sugar

4 large egg yolks

1 teaspoon vanilla extract

Preparation

In a medium saucepan, heat the heavy cream and brewed coffee over medium heat until it begins to simmer. Remove from heat.

Add the chopped dark chocolate to the saucepan and stir until completely melted and smooth.

In a separate bowl, whisk together the sugar and egg yolks until well combined.

Slowly pour the chocolate mixture into the egg mixture, whisking constantly to prevent the eggs from scrambling.

Reintroduce the mixture to the pan, and simmer it there over low heat, continually swirling, until it slightly thickens and coats the back of a spoon. This should take about 5 minutes.

Remove from heat and stir in the vanilla extract.

Pour the mixture into individual serving dishes or ramekins.

Set after at least 4 hours in the refrigerator.

Serve chilled and garnish with whipped cream or chocolate shavings, if desired.

2.Espresso Brownies

Ingredients

1 cup unsalted butter

2 cups granulated sugar

4 large eggs

1 teaspoon vanilla extract

1/2 cup all-purpose flour

1/4 cup cocoa powder

1/4 teaspoon salt

1/4 cup brewed espresso or strong coffee

1 cup semisweet chocolate chips

Preparation

Grease a 9x13-inch baking dish and preheat your oven to 350°F (175°C).

In a microwave-safe bowl, melt the butter.

Add the sugar and mix thoroughly.

One at a time, add the eggs, thoroughly combining after each addition..Stir in the vanilla extract.

Mix the flour, cocoa powder, and salt in another basin.

Add the dry ingredients a little at a time while mixing the butter mixture.

Add the freshly made espresso or strong coffee and stir.

Fold in the chocolate chips.

Spread the batter evenly after adding it to the baking dish that has been prepared.

A toothpick inserted into the center should come out with a few moist crumbs after baking for about 25 to 30 minutes.

After taking the brownies out of the oven, let them cool fully before cutting them into squares.

3.Coffee Crème Brûlée
Ingredients

2 cups heavy cream

1/4 cup brewed coffee, cooled

1/2 cup granulated sugar, divided

4 large egg yolks

1 teaspoon vanilla extract

Extra sugar for caramelizing

Preparation

Preheat your oven to 325°F (160°C).

In a saucepan, heat the heavy cream, brewed coffee, and 1/4 cup of sugar over medium heat until it starts to simmer. Remove from heat.

In a mixing bowl, whisk together the egg yolks, remaining 1/4 cup of sugar, and vanilla extract until well combined.

Using a whisk to keep the mixture from curdling, slowly pour the hot cream mixture into the egg mixture.

Strain the mixture through a fine-mesh sieve into a pouring pitcher or bowl.

Place six ramekins in a baking dish and divide the custard mixture evenly among them.

Fill the baking dish with hot water until it reaches about halfway up the sides of the ramekins.

Transfer the baking pan with care to the prepared oven, then bake.

4.Coffee Panna Cotta

Ingredients

2 cups heavy cream

1/2 cup granulated sugar

2 teaspoons instant coffee

2 teaspoons gelatin powder

1/4 cup cold water

1 teaspoon vanilla extract

Preparation

The heavy cream and sugar should be combined in a pan. Occasionally stir while you heat over medium heat until the sugar dissolves.

In a small bowl, mix the instant coffee with a little bit of hot water to dissolve it completely.

Add the coffee mixture to the saucepan and stir well.

In a separate small bowl, sprinkle the gelatin powder over the cold water and let it sit for about 5 minutes to bloom.

Once the gelatin has bloomed, place the bowl in a microwave and heat it for about 15-20 seconds until the gelatin is completely dissolved. Alternatively, you can heat the gelatin mixture on the stovetop using low heat.

Pour the gelatin mixture into the saucepan with the coffee cream mixture and stir well.

Add the vanilla extract after turning off the heat in the saucepan.

Pour the mixture into individual serving dishes or ramekins.

The panna cotta should be chilled for at least 4 hours or until set. Let it come to room temperature first.

Once set, serve the coffee panna cotta chilled. You can garnish it with whipped cream or chocolate shavings, if desired.

5.Coffee Cheesecake
Ingredients for the crust

1 1/2 cups graham cracker crumbs

1/4 cup melted butter

1/4 cup granulated sugar

Ingredients for the filling

2 (8 oz) packages cream cheese, softened

1 cup granulated sugar

2 tablespoons all-purpose flour

2 tablespoons instant coffee, dissolved in 1 tablespoon hot water

1 teaspoon vanilla extract

3 eggs

Preparation

Preheat the oven to 325°F (160°C). A 9-inch springform pan should be greased and left aside.

In a bowl, mix together the graham cracker crumbs, melted butter, and granulated sugar until well combined.

Press the crumb mixture firmly into the bottom of the prepared springform pan to form the crust.

Cream the cream cheese in a sizable mixing bowl until it is smooth and creamy.

Add the granulated sugar, flour, dissolved instant coffee, and vanilla extract to the cream cheese. Beat until well combined and smooth.

One at a time, add the eggs, beating thoroughly after each addition.

Over the springform pan's shell, pour the cream cheese mixture.

Use a spatula or the back of a spoon to level the top.

Place the springform pan in the preheated oven and bake for about 50-60 minutes or until the center is set and the edges are lightly golden.

After removing the cheesecake from the oven, give it a 10-minute cooling period in the pan.

Run a knife around the edges of the pan to loosen the cheesecake, then remove the sides of the springform pan.

Allow the cheesecake to cool completely, then refrigerate for at least 4 hours or overnight before serving.

Serve chilled and garnish with whipped cream or chocolate curls, if desired.

6.Coffee Ice Cream

Ingredients

2 cups heavy cream

1 cup whole milk

3/4 cup granulated sugar

Using 1 tablespoon of hot water, dissolve 2 teaspoons of instant coffee.

1 teaspoon vanilla extract

Preparation

In a mixing bowl, whisk together the heavy cream, whole milk, granulated sugar, dissolved instant coffee, and vanilla extract until the sugar is fully dissolved.

As directed by the manufacturer, pour the ingredients into an ice cream machine and churn.

Transfer the ice cream to a container with a lid when it has a soft-serve consistency.

Put the container in the freezer and wait at least 4 hours or overnight for the ice cream to set.

When ready to serve, scoop the coffee ice cream into bowls or cones and enjoy!

Note: You can pour the mixture into a shallow dish and freeze it if you don't have an ice cream machine. Every 30 minutes, remove the dish from the freezer and stir vigorously to break up any ice crystals. Repeat this process for about 3-4 hours until the ice cream reaches the desired consistency.

7.Mocha Cupcakes

Ingredients

1 ¾ cups all-purpose flour

1 ½ teaspoons baking powder

½ teaspoon baking soda

¼ teaspoon salt

½ cup unsweetened cocoa powder

1 cup granulated sugar

½ cup unsalted butter, softened

2 large eggs

1 teaspoon vanilla extract

1 cup buttermilk

½ cup strong brewed coffee, cooled

Preparation

Preheat the oven to 350°F (175°C) and line a cupcake pan with paper liners.

Mix the flour, baking powder, baking soda, salt, and cocoa powder in a medium bowl.

Cream the sugar and butter in a different, big dish until they are light and creamy.

One at a time, add the eggs, beating thoroughly after each addition. Add the vanilla extract and stir.

Alternate adding the buttermilk and flour mixtures to the butter mixture gradually. The flour mixture should be added first and last.

Mix in the cold brewed coffee until the batter is smooth and well combined.

Spoon the batter into the prepared cupcake liners, filling each about 2/3 full.

A toothpick put into the center of a cupcake should come out clean after baking it for 18 to 20 minutes.

The cupcakes should be taken out of the oven and allowed to cool for a few minutes in the pan before being moved to a wire rack to finish cooling.

Once cooled, you can frost the cupcakes with your favorite mocha frosting or dust them with powdered sugar. Enjoy!

8. Coffee Macarons

Ingredients

For the macarons:

1 ¾ cups powdered sugar

1 cup almond flour

3 large egg whites, at room temperature

¼ cup granulated sugar

2 tablespoons instant coffee powder

For the coffee buttercream filling:

½ cup unsalted butter, softened

1 ½ cups powdered sugar

2 teaspoons instant coffee powder

2 tablespoons heavy cream

Preparation

Line a baking sheet with parchment paper and prepare a piping bag with a round tip.

In a medium bowl, sift together the powdered sugar, almond flour, and instant coffee powder. Set aside.

In a large mixing bowl, beat the egg whites until frothy.

Gradually incorporate the sugar crystals while mixing the mixture until firm peaks form.

Gently fold the dry ingredients into the egg white mixture until fully incorporated. Be careful not to overmix.

Transfer the batter to the prepared piping bag and pipe small rounds onto the lined baking sheet.

To get rid of any air bubbles, tap the baking sheet on the counter a few times. Let the macarons sit at room temperature for about 30 minutes until a skin forms on the surface.

Preheat the oven to 325°F (160°C) and bake the macarons for 12-15 minutes until they are set and easily lift off the parchment paper. On the baking sheet, allow them to finish cooling.

In a mixing bowl, cream the softened butter until smooth. Gradually add the powdered sugar and instant coffee powder, and continue mixing until well combined.

Add the heavy cream and beat until the buttercream is light and fluffy.

Match the macaron shells in pairs of similar size. Pipe a dollop of coffee buttercream onto one shell and gently sandwich it with another.

To let the flavors mingle, place the filled macarons in an airtight container and place in the refrigerator for at least 24 hours. Bring them to room temperature before serving. Enjoy!

9.Coffee Walnut Cake
Ingredients

2 cups all-purpose flour

2 teaspoons baking powder

½ teaspoon baking soda

¼ teaspoon salt

½ cup unsalted butter, softened

1 cup granulated sugar

2 large eggs

1 teaspoon vanilla extract

1 cup strong brewed coffee, cooled

½ cup milk

1 cup chopped walnuts

For the coffee frosting:

1 ½ cups heavy cream

2 tablespoons instant coffee powder

¼ cup powdered sugar

For the coffee glaze:

1 cup powdered sugar

2 tablespoons strong brewed coffee, cooled

Preparation

Prepare a 9-inch round cake pan with oil and preheat the oven to 350°F (175°C).

Mix the flour, baking soda, baking powder, and salt in a medium bowl.

Butter and sugar are combined in a sizable basin and creamed until frothy.

One at a time, add the eggs, beating thoroughly after each addition. Stir in the vanilla extract.

Mix in the cold brewed coffee and milk until combined.

Mix just till incorporated after adding the dry ingredients in small amounts to the wet ones.

Fold in the chopped walnuts.

Fill the prepared cake pan with the batter, then use a spatula to smooth the top.

A toothpick put into the center of the cake should come out clean after baking for 30-35 minutes.

The cake should be taken out of the oven and left to cool for 10 minutes in the pan. After that, move it to a wire rack to finish cooling.

For the coffee frosting, in a mixing bowl, combine the heavy cream, instant coffee powder, and powdered sugar. Beat until stiff peaks form.

Once the cake has cooled, spread the coffee frosting over the top and sides of the cake.

For the coffee glaze, whisk together the powdered sugar and brewed coffee until smooth. The cake should be glazed and drizzled with it.

Optional: Garnish the cake with additional chopped walnuts.

Slice and serve the delicious coffee walnut cake.

10. Coffee Biscotti

Ingredients

2 cups all-purpose flour

1 teaspoon baking powder

1/4 teaspoon salt

1/2 cup unsalted butter, softened

3/4 cup granulated sugar

2 large eggs

2 teaspoons instant coffee granules

1 teaspoon vanilla extract

1/2 cup chopped walnuts (optional)

Preparation

Preheat your oven to 350°F (175°C). Use parchment paper to cover a baking sheet.

Mix the salt, baking powder, and flour in a medium-sized bowl. Place aside.

Cream the butter and sugar in a different, big bowl until they are light and creamy.

One at a time, beat the eggs thoroughly after each addition before adding them to the butter mixture.

Dissolve the instant coffee granules in 1 tablespoon of hot water, then add it to the butter mixture along with the vanilla extract. Mix well.

Mix just till incorporated after adding the dry ingredients in small amounts to the wet ones. Fold in the chopped walnuts, if desired.

Divide the dough in half and shape each portion into a 12-inch long log on the prepared baking sheet, spacing them apart.

Bake in the preheated oven for 25-30 minutes, or until the logs are firm and golden brown.

The logs should be taken out of the oven and left to cool for 15 minutes on the baking sheet.

Reduce the oven temperature to 325°F (165°C).

Transfer the logs to a cutting board and slice them diagonally into 1/2-inch thick slices.

The biscotti slices should be crisp and dry by the time you put them back on the baking sheet and bake them for an additional 10-15 minutes.

After taking them out of the oven, let them cool completely before serving.

11.Coffee Bread Pudding
Ingredients

4 cups stale bread cubes

2 cups whole milk

1/2 cup strong brewed coffee

1/2 cup granulated sugar

3 large eggs

1 teaspoon vanilla extract

1/4 teaspoon ground cinnamon

1/4 teaspoon salt

1/2 cup raisins (optional)

Preparation

Preheat your oven to 350°F (175°C). Grease a 9x9-inch baking dish.

In a large bowl, combine the bread cubes, milk, and brewed coffee. Let it sit for 10 minutes, allowing the bread to absorb the liquid.

In a separate bowl, whisk together the sugar, eggs, vanilla extract, cinnamon, and salt until well combined.

Pour the egg mixture over the soaked bread cubes, stirring gently to evenly distribute the mixture.

If desired, fold in the raisins.

Transfer the bread mixture to the greased baking dish, spreading it out evenly.

Bake in the preheated oven for 40-45 minutes, or until the bread pudding is set and the top is golden brown.

Before serving, remove from the oven and allow to cool slightly. Serve warm or at room temperature.

12. Coffee Cream Pie

Ingredients

For the crust:

1 1/2 cups graham cracker crumbs

1/4 cup granulated sugar

1/2 cup unsalted butter, melted

For the filling:

1 1/2 cups heavy cream

1/2 cup strong brewed coffee

1/2 cup granulated sugar

1/4 cup cornstarch

1/4 teaspoon salt

4 large egg yolks

2 tablespoons unsalted butter

1 teaspoon vanilla extract

For the topping:

1 cup heavy cream

2 tablespoons powdered sugar

Cocoa powder or chocolate shavings for garnish (optional)

Preparation

In a medium-sized bowl, combine the graham cracker crumbs, sugar, and melted butter. The crumbs should be evenly covered after mixing.

Press the crumb mixture into the bottom and up the sides of a 9-inch pie dish to form the crust. Press it firmly with the back of a spoon.

While you prepare the filling, chill the crust in the refrigerator.

In a saucepan, combine the heavy cream, brewed coffee, sugar, cornstarch, and salt.

Mixture should be thoroughly blended and smooth after whisking.

Cook the mixture, stirring frequently, in the saucepan over medium heat until it thickens and gently boils.

The egg yolks should be well beaten in a different bowl. Pour half of the hot cream mixture into the egg yolks slowly while continuously whisking to temper the eggs.

Whipping continuously, add the tempered egg mixture back into the pot with the remaining cream mixture.

Continue cooking the mixture over medium heat, stirring constantly, until it thickens to a pudding-like consistency.

Once the butter has melted and been thoroughly mixed, turn off the heat and add the vanilla essence.

Pour the filling into the chilled pie crust, smoothing the top with a spatula.

Cover the pie with plastic wrap, ensuring that the plastic wrap touches the surface of the filling to prevent a skin from forming.

Refrigerate the pie for at least 4 hours or overnight until it is fully chilled and set.

Just before serving, prepare the topping by whipping the heavy cream and powdered sugar together until soft peaks form.

Spread the whipped cream over the chilled pie, and if desired, sprinkle cocoa powder or chocolate shavings on top for garnish.

Slice and serve the coffee cream pie chilled. Enjoy!

CONCLUSION

*I*n "The Complete Coffee Cookbook," we embarked on a journey through the rich and aromatic world of coffee, exploring its diverse flavors, brewing methods, and the delightful recipes that can be created using this beloved beverage. Throughout this book, we discovered that coffee is more than just a morning pick-me-up; it is a versatile ingredient that can elevate both sweet and savory dishes to new heights.

One of the highlights of this book was undoubtedly the collection of coffee-infused recipes. We delved into the realm of breakfast delights, discovering how coffee can add depth and richness to pancakes, muffins, and granolas. And of course, we indulged in the world of desserts, where coffee can be the star of luscious cakes, creamy mousses, and decadent ice creams.

"The Complete Coffee Cookbook" is not only a guide to brewing and cooking with coffee; it is an invitation to embrace the sensory pleasures and rituals associated with this beloved beverage. From the first intoxicating whiff of freshly ground beans to the satisfying sip of a perfectly brewed cup, coffee engages all our senses and brings joy to our daily lives.

*A*s we conclude this culinary journey, let us remember that coffee is more than just a drink; it is a catalyst for connection and conversation. It brings people together, sparks creativity, and creates moments of warmth and comfort. Whether enjoyed alone in peaceful solitude or shared with loved ones, coffee has the power to nourish both body and soul.

I hope this book has inspired you to embark on your own coffee adventures, to experiment with new flavors, and to infuse your culinary creations with the magic of coffee. May it serve as a constant companion in your kitchen, unlocking a world of delicious possibilities. So grab your favorite mug, brew a cup of your preferred coffee, and let your imagination run wild as you continue to explore the endless possibilities of "The Complete Coffee Cookbook."

Cheers to the perfect cup of coffee and the incredible culinary experiences it brings!

Made in United States
Orlando, FL
06 December 2023

40336362R00046